SUCCESS STARTS HERE
THE BASICS TO A SUCCESSFUL LIFE

Jermaine L. Jenkins

AuthorHouse™
1663 Liberty Drive
Bloomington, IN 47403
www.authorhouse.com
Phone: 1-800-839-8640

Published by AuthorHouse 2/21/2013

ISBN: 978-1-4772-1045-1 (sc)
ISBN: 978-1-4772-1044-4 (hc)
ISBN: 978-1-4772-1043-7 (e)

Library of Congress Control Number: 2012909089

This book is dedicated to all the people who have overcome negative situations and turned them into positive life accomplishments. You too can be successful if you dream, have a plan, and let nothing deter you from achieving your goals.

Contents

Introduction ix

Special Thanks to These Special People and Organizations xi

A Picture Does Mean a Thousand Words. xiii

Meeting Jermaine Jenkins xiv

Chapter 1: Where it all Started. 1

Chapter 2: South Forrest Elementary School 5

Chapter 3: Forrest County Agricultural High School. 7

Chapter 4: My Early Years in the Marine Corps 9

Chapter 5: New Peers and College 13

Chapter 6: The Military and College Continued 17

Chapter 7: Why You Should Consider Joining the Military
            and Tips on Promotions 21

Chapter 8: Military College-Assistance Programs 25

Chapter 9: Embassy Duty in Kabul, Afghanistan 27

Chapter 10: Returning from Kabul, Afghanistan 29

Chapter 11: Meeting Presidents and Working at Embassies 33

Chapter 12: Exposure to Other Countries and People 39

Chapter 13: Mentors: Everyone Needs One 43

Chapter 14: Financial Investment 47

Chapter 15: Keeping Up with the Joneses 51

Chapter 16: An Emergency Account. 53

Chapter 17: Managing Your Credit Score 55

Chapter 18: Taxes 61

Chapter 19: Job Versus Career 65

Chapter 20: Are You a Leader or a Follower?. 67

Chapter 21: Public Speaking. 71

Chapter 22: The Importance of Physical and Mental Fitness. . . .73

Chapter 23: Parents Are Crippling Their Children "The
             Crutch, Bailout and Accountability Theory" 83

Chapter 24: Preparing for the Mission in Combat and Life 85

Conclusion 89

Introduction

N ever in a million years would I have thought that I would shake hands with two United States Presidents, Bill Clinton and Barack Obama, and Former Secretary of State Condoleezza Rice. My life and career in the United States Marine Corps has taken me around the world. I have had many good and bad experiences in life, but I learned from them all. I also have made some common mistakes to which most people can relate. In this book I will recount my mistakes and travels and how I learned from all of these experiences.

I was a teen parent in high school and it was said that I would never amount to anything in life. I was never asked about going to college, never taught about the importance of a good credit score. I was never taught how to manage my money or how to file income taxes. I learned all of these things late in my life and now life is great.

You will see the methods I used to accomplish a master's degree and success in my career. Following my Life Learning Tips will give you the basic tools you need to have a successful career and to become a great mentor.

I want you to know as well that part of the proceeds from this book will go to disabled veterans.

Success Starts Here is my first book. I poured my heart into this project, for which reason I hope that you will enjoy it.

My thanks to everyone who purchased this book!

Yours truly,
Jermaine L. Jenkins

Special Thanks to These Special People and Organizations

Tangela Jenkins (Wife)

MARINE CORPS, ARMY, NAVY, AIR FORCE, COAST GUARD,

Johnny Dupree, Ph.D. (Mayor, Hattiesburg, Mississippi)

William Jones (Retired Gunnery Sergeant, Marine Corps)

Vanessa Jones (Judge, Hattiesburg, Mississippi)

Daryl Stillings (Sergeant Major, Marine Corps)

Carl Sheppard (Principal, Forrest County Agricultural High School)

Coach Perry and Mrs. Wheat (Forrest County Agricultural High School)

Coach Riley (South Forrest Elementary School)

Coach Dolan (Forrest County Agricultural High School)

Mark Burrell (Major, Marine Corps)

Oddie and Alvin Jenkins (Mother and Father)

Christopher Combs (Sergeant Major, Marine Corps)

Herman Kirkland (Master Sergeant, Marine Corps)

Willie Heppard, III (Retired Gunnery Sergeant, Marine Corps)

Herbert Kennedy (Retired Gunnery Sergeant, Marine Corps)

Tracy Clemons (Retired Staff Sergeant, Marine Corps)

Mike Elliot (Retired Gunnery Sergeant/Civil Service)

Teresa Mullen (Retired Gunnery Sergeant/Civil Service)

Robert Williamson (Sergeant Major, Marine Corps)

Michael Mimms (Retired Master Sergeant, Marine Corps)

Howard Bouldin (Pastor)

Linda Swan (Mother-in-Law and Mentor)

Curtis Mason (Lieutenant Colonel, Marine Corps)

Richard and Amy Sroka (Master Sergeant, Marine Corps and Hinds Community College Representative)

Michael Smith (Gunnery Sergeant, Marine Corps and Gym Partner)

Squares, Nobles and Stars

Alpha's, Kappa's, Omega's, Sigma's, Iota Phi Theta

AKA's, Delta's, Zeta's, Sigma Gamma Rho

Priscilla Jenkins (Friend and Supporter)

Harold Moore (Family Friend and Retired Gunnery Sergeant)

A Picture Does Mean a Thousand Words

In January 2000 I saw a picture of four highly successful officers in the United States Marine Corps on a poster. It was hanging on a wall in my headquarters building. The men looked very professional in their uniforms and had a rewarding career, life, and salary. I asked myself what I needed to do in order to achieve such success.

I knew that each of the men had a four-year college degree, great leadership abilities, a strong work ethic, discipline, and good public-speaking skills. I decided to emulate their leadership traits. I started and completed my college degree while working on all areas of leadership. I quickly learned that following the example of successful people can lead to personal success.

Overall, I have learned that success has to be earned. You have to want it and want it bad. You also must be willing to make sacrifices. Now sit back and enjoy this inspirational book based on my life experiences. It contains something for everyone that will help people to grow and reach their highest goals.

Meeting Jermaine Jenkins

I was born in Hattiesburg, Mississippi, in June 1974 but raised in McLaurin. In 1991 my cousin told me that family members were saying, "Jermaine is becoming a father in the eleventh grade. He won't amount to anything." The scariest part for me involved explaining to my dad while he was changing out of his Army uniform that his youngest son was having a child while still in high school. After I had quietly explained the pregnancy, he said: "Son, every day you will carry her books and support her. Your mom and I will work to assist and support you." In February 1992 I became the father of a beautiful girl. While others looked down on me, I was wondering how I was going to make it. I felt embarrassed and unsure of myself.

In May 1993 I graduated from Forrest County Agricultural High School. The next year I decided to join the United States Marine Corps. One of my cousins asked, "Are you sure you can make it through Paris Island Boot Camp?" The comment made me determined to succeed.

My mom and dad never owned their own home while I was growing up, but we made the best of whatever we lived in. Most of time that was trailer homes. Throughout my life I have faced many difficult challenges and negative experiences that could have led me down the path to drugs, gangs, and crime. Most of my friends were in gangs and sold drugs, but fortunately I joined the military.

Around the age of 27, while in the Marine Corps, I met some peers who profoundly changed my outlook. I started to believe in myself and learned that I could do anything to which I put my mind. This change in perspective immeasurably enhanced my career in the Marine Corps as well as my family life. I now aspire to teach others what it takes to be successful in life. Here is my story.

May 2012. Jermaine Jenkins is ready for business and continued success with hard work and dedication.

Chapter 1
Where it all Started

McLaurin, Mississippi, is a small rural town, but we had many great days there. I was a mama's baby, and she carried me everywhere she went. I was such an active kid that she did not trust anybody to baby-sit me besides herself and a few select others. One summer, while we were playing near a cement ditch, I fell in and knocked out my two front teeth. I cannot remember the incident, but my mom has the pictures to prove that I was a daredevil. Perhaps that's why I am in the United States Marine Corps and certified to jump from airplanes.

My dad also grew up in McLaurin. He is a handsome fellow who loves his family. He served in the National Guard for 23 years at Camp Shelby Army Base. Dad worked hard and made sure that we had what we needed for school and everyday living.

We were not a rich family and, as already mentioned, never owned our own home. We moved several times when I was a kid. I recall visiting my friend Tommy Shomake, with whom I played basketball in grammar school. I never knew what his mother and father did for jobs, but I do remember them having a nice big house where we would hang out before games. I was never jealous of the success of my friend's family, but I knew I wanted a taste of it.

Another friend, John Davis, was also from a well established family. They had an attractive brick home with a pool and other amenities that my family could not afford. Spending time at their home motivated me to work hard so that one day I could have my own family and nice things.

One summer, after baseball ended, our team went to Peps Point Water Park for a post-season celebration. I almost drowned following some friends across the deep water. Not long afterwards John Davis family invited me to their house and told me to jump into their swimming pool and move my legs in a bicycle motion to resurface. I gathered my nerve, jumped into the middle of the pool, and for a second while under water started to panic, but I remembered what they had said. I paddled my legs and hands and came back to the surface. I had overcome my first major obstacle in life. Little did I know that I was on my way.

There will always be some challenges in life that we fear, but you have to overcome your fear. Do this by asking for help. Conquering your fear in certain areas will boost your confidence in others. When you confront your next obstacle, reflect back on your first challenge and how you overcame it. Use it as motivation to get over the new one. Never be afraid to ask for help, but make sure that the people whose help you are asking are qualified to assist you.

Life Learning Tip

I read a few years ago that three young African American males were walking near a stream when the ground near the creek collapsed, causing the boys to fall into the water. Two of the boys died because they did not know how to swim. This same situation almost happened to me, but I did something about it.

Most non-swimmers fear that when they go into a body of water they will never come up again. You can overcome your fear by trusting qualified swim instructors, but first you must have faith in yourself to accomplish this goal.

When I invite many of my African American friends to join my wife and me on a couples cruise, many decline due to not knowing how to swim. You should not miss out on great experiences because you cannot overcome a fear of swimming. You and your kids will need to learn how to swim if they intend to join the Marine Corps, Army, Coast Guard, or Navy. Have faith in yourself and learn to enjoy the great sport of swimming.

My Father, Alvin Jenkins

My dad would have loved to provide our family with a house like those in which Tommy and James lived, but he could not. Perhaps it was because he had bad credit, did not make enough money, or had a serious alcohol problem that consumed much of his income.

Alcohol abuse ruined the possibility of many well-paying jobs for my father. It also destroyed his marriage and caused our family to suffer. My dad, whom I love dearly, could have been a great man if he had put the bottle down and concentrated more on teaching me and my siblings valuable lessons to prepare us for success in life.

Life Learning Tip

Many people blame the outcome of their lives on parental example. I would agree with them to an extent. After fathering a child in the eleventh grade and hearing that some family members had dismissed my future prospects, I learned to turn negative things into positive outcomes. I do a lot of mentoring these days about not using drugs and not attending college. Why? Because no one talked to me about these important issues. Read this book and learn how to be successful.

My Mother, Oddie Jenkins

My mom grew up in Cleveland, Ohio. My dad met her during high school, and their relationship blossomed into marriage and three kids. Though not a college graduate, my mom worked very hard as well as our dad to make sure that we had what we needed. Before I left for Boot Camp, I remember her working at six different places as a cook. My fondest memory is that of her being hired to manage a Waffle House type of restaurant. The eatery was losing revenue, however, and she didn't know how to turn it around, not having a college degree in marketing or business. The lack of such necessary skills caused her to lose a managerial position. I recall how sad she was when she was replaced. I was 14 years old then, but I was learning about life from the outside looking in.

Life Learning Tip

From this experience I learned that business is all about performance. You have to perform every day because there is always someone out there who would be glad to have your position. You need to learn everything possible about your job. One way to do this is to take some college courses in your area of expertise. Earning a degree in your occupation increases your chance of earning more. To be a great employee and manager, you should combine on-the-job training with a college degree or certificate program. Welcome appointment to supervisory positions and ask for greater responsibilities in your field of work or endeavor.

Chapter 2

South Forrest
Elementary School

South Forrest Elementary was a great school with wonderful teachers. Few African Americans were enrolled there, but for the most part everyone got along well. I was in the first grade with my cousins Thomas, Preston, Chris, and Terry. I do not remember a lot of the work back then, but I do recall Terry looking at my report card and saying I had failed. I was devastated when I realized that I would not be entering second grade with my cousins. I didn't understand then that everything happens for a reason. It was while repeating first grade the next year that I met the good friends mentioned in the preceding chapter.

I never considered myself a smart student, being average in most subjects and below average in others such as math. One semester during eighth grade I failed math, causing me to miss the basketball playoffs. I always cared about my grades but simply was not good at math. Unfortunately my family did not help me with the subject at home, probably because they might not have known how to solve the problems either and thought it was the teacher's job, not theirs, to make sure we passed. Usually, however, the math teachers did not have the time to spend with one kid when they had a whole class to worry about. What I really needed was a tutor. I liked all of my teachers at South Forrest Elementary and do not fault them for anything, but I do think that teachers need to devote more attention to students who need help rather than the standouts.

Life Learning Tip

Parents, you must monitor your children's grades if you expect them to have a chance at college and potentially a better life. It is extremely important that you be involved in their homework and make sure they are turning in their work on time. You thus will know early on whether your child is weak in a particular subject. He or she then has time to get help from a teacher, family member, or tutor.

I remember envying my friends who were taking accelerated classes. I used to say to myself that I wished I were as smart as Kelli Roane, Brad Simmons, or Trey Morris. Most of these classmates had parents who were actively involved in their children's education; because of their academic achievement, they also enjoyed the support of teachers. That is fine, of course, but we cannot forget about those kids in our nation's classrooms who desperately need help.

America owes all children more individualized attention in school. We have to identify problems early on with kids and get them help, because doing so will strengthen our communities and nation. We also need smaller classes so that kids can receive the help they need.

Teachers, I ask that you set up remedial programs for your troubled students. Try to reach out to parents and confer with them about their children's grades. Give parents a game plan for how to get their kids back on track. One thing I understand from firsthand experience is that not all of us can be outstanding in math, science, and English, but if we try hard enough we can at least be reasonably proficient.

Chapter 3

Forrest County Agricultural High School

I loved high school and had an outstanding time at Forrest County Agricultural. The principal, Carl Sheppard, ran a tight ship and cared about all his students. Our superintendent, Mr. Lowery, was a well mannered and low-key individual. These two gentlemen made an awesome team.

I worked hard in high school to maintain my grades, primarily so that I could continue to play sports. I was doing okay in most subjects, but math was still difficult for me. During my junior year I joined Student Council Club. At our meetings we talked about school policies and functions such as homecoming. Because every year the football cheerleaders and homecoming queen were white, I suggested that we needed a change in policy. To my surprise it happened! This was my first taste of politics, and I loved it.

Throughout high school I do not recall ever thinking about becoming a doctor, policeman, firefighter, or any of the other professionals that kids always say they want some day to be. No one ever encouraged me to have such aspirations. Most of the smart kids belonged to the Beta Club, where the prospect of college was a normal topic of conversation. Parents and teachers alike should urge *all* students to pursue higher education based upon their level of academic preparation and ability.

During my senior year I started to worry about what I was going to do after graduation and how I was going to support my daughter. So far my parents had helped to raise her, and I had been working during the summers at Camp Shelby National Guard Base. My high school then took all the seniors on a visit to Pearl River Community College. While there athletes could try out for the football team, so I went just for that opportunity. Because I had not been recruited and because I did not have good grades, college had never crossed my mind. In the next chapter you will discover how my life took a new turn.

Life Learning Tip

Parents, stress to your kids how important it is to acquire a college education and the skills that America needs. Over the span of a lifetime a college graduate will earn approximately one million dollars more than a person without a degree. Too often parents in poorer communities do not encourage their children to pursue college and a professional education. Don't cheat your kids by not giving them the best advice possible to be successful in life. There is a huge difference between a career and a job. Give your children a chance to have a better life than you.

Chapter 4

My Early Years
in the Marine Corps

After high school I had to find a job to support my daughter and myself. I was afraid that I would end up with a nine-to-five job and make barely enough money to stay afloat. Because some of my close friends were joining the Navy, I decided to follow their example. After not doing so well on the screening test the first time, I retook it. Then the Marine Corps and Army recruiters called me. The Army sales pitch was nice, but Marine Corps recruiters can sell you a broken-down truck from a junkyard. In short, I signed up. Little did I know eighteen years ago that this would be the best decision of my life.

I joined the Marine Corps in February 1994, leaving for training at Paris Island Boot Camp the same month. It was, shall we say, highly challenging. There were many days when I asked myself, "What am I doing here?" Marine Corps training is the real deal. You probably have seen the commercial about "The Few, the Proud, the Marines." That truly does sum it up. After three months at Paris Island, I came out a new person.

In September 1994 I received orders to report to El Toro, California, for duty. Upon arriving at Los Angeles International Airport, I was amazed by all the different nationalities of people there. Coming from Hattiesburg, Mississippi, I had been used to seeing mostly African Americans and Caucasians. In the City of Angels I was happy to see that everyone was getting along and that interracial dating was more accepted here than back at home.

California opened my eyes to a whole new world. I had never seen shopping malls so sprawling until I visited LA's Fox Hill Mall. I'm sure that everyone knew I was a tourist because I kept looking up at the skyscrapers and taking pictures. I also was agog at seeing mansions built on the rims of cliffs. In Hollywood I touched the stars of Michael Jackson, Mel Gibson, and Danny Glover. I saw the homes of Morgan Freeman, Sylvester Stallone, and other movie moguls. In sum, I felt as though I were living in a dream.

In 1995 I left California for a year in Okinawa, Japan. There I encountered an entirely new culture and even learned how to speak some Japanese. Then, while in Japan, my unit went to Thailand for two months of training. At the end of the day we enjoyed local cuisine and exchanged stories with the Royal Thai Marines, who showed us around their country. A lot of the indigenous people did not have running or clean water. I also saw ramshackle houses that were barely standing. I quickly realized how blessed we are in the United States. Appreciate what you have and thank God every day for it.

In 1996 I married my daughter's mother and moved to Oceanside, California, site of the Camp Pendleton Marine Base. My family and I lived there for three years. My two young daughters, Charmane and Quanisha, got to see a new state and even learned a little Spanish. Because Oceanside is located about fifty miles from San Diego, I had a chance while there to watch the San Diego Chargers play. I also went to a San Diego bar to watch our Hattiesburg, Mississippi, resident and soon-to-be Hall of Famer, Brett Favre, receive his Super Bowl ring.

In 1998 my unit was ordered to Kuwait because of Saddam Hussein's military aggression. We were put on civilian ships headed for the Middle East. I liked being on board ship after I got over the initial motion sickness. During the day we sometimes saw dolphins and stingrays swimming near the ship. You're at peace when on the ocean, seeing nothing but water for miles.

After a few weeks of sailing, our ship pulled into Bahrain for some relaxation and down time. Bahrain was extremely hot but had some great shopping malls. We also toured the local gold markets and looked at some beautiful homes. Once again I was in a new country.

After one month on duty with Operation Vigilant Warrior, we were ordered home via airplane. One of our refueling stops was Rota, Spain. While there we had engine problems and had to spend the next three days on our own in the town. I never thought that life could be so great! A young Mississippi guy was in Spain seeing beautiful women and eating delicious food. I visited three countries on the trip home and quickly realized that I was a good fit for the military and that it was a good fit for me.

During these first six years in the Marine Corps I was not saving any money. I was having a great time, but my family and I were living from paycheck to paycheck. Five days before payday I typically had about thirty dollars left to support a wife and two kids. We usually had Hamburger Helper for dinner during those times. I was only an E-4 corporal and at that rank did not make much money. In other words, I was stuck in the same economic trap that I had known while growing up in Mississippi. Something needed to change.

Chapter 5

New Peers and College

I arrived at the Marine Base in Albany, Georgia, in January 2000. At the post I met my new peers and knew right away that this was going to be a good assignment. After being there for just a few months, I ran into an old buddy named Gunnery Sergeant William Jones, whom I had met in Hattiesburg when he was a recruiter. I also became friends with Samuel Monk, Richard Sroka, and Daryl Stilling. All of these Marines were enrolled at Hinds Community College.

One day Samuel and Richard told me that I should start taking college courses because eventually I would have to retire from the military. I was scared to death because I had not made the best grades in high school and had failed the first grade. These gentlemen, however, encouraged me to get a college education. It was the first time that someone expressed to me how important it was to obtain a college degree. They told me that it would open many doors and enhance my chances for future success.

After gathering my courage, I applied at Hinds Community College and started with one class, Introduction to Criminal Justice. I loved the course and received a final grade of A. I have always had an interest in criminal justice as well as in state politics.

Working and studying very hard, I started to believe in myself. After about eighteen months in college, I was inducted into Phi Theta Kappa, an intercollegiate honor society, for maintaining a grade-point average

(GPA) of 3.5 or higher. My family was able to attend my induction. This was a great day for us all.

I graduated *magna cum laude* from Hinds Community College in December 2001 with a GPA of 3.7. Both I and many others never thought that the teenager who became a father in high school and who never earned good grades back then would be receiving a college degree with honors. It was one of the proudest days in my life. Receiving my two-year degree only made me hungrier for more knowledge of criminal justice and politics. Knowing that I wanted my bachelor's degree next, I was determined to achieve this goal.

Life Learning Tip

No matter what your grades were in elementary and secondary school, you still have a chance to receive a college education. Some people are intimidated by the word "college," remembering hard classes in high school. They start to doubt themselves, and before you know it they have given up their dream of a career and a better quality of life for their children.

Family members, you need to stand behind your college students and support them in their studies. Remember also that when your spouse or child gets that degree it is better for everyone. If you have a child who is frightened by the prospect of college; please explain the benefits of a good education and remind him or her to stay focused on the prize.

True Story

A few months after receiving my degree, my brother Demond and I were en route to Leesburg Church of Christ in Leesburg, Georgia. It was about 6:45 p.m. and getting dark. I was driving my 1998 Ford Expedition with 22" rims. Spotting a state trooper parked on the median ahead, I slowed down to make sure that I was not over the speed limit. Five minutes later I noticed the trooper behind me with his lights flashing. After I pulled over, he came up to my SUV and said, "You know why I stopped you, right?" I said that I didn't. He then claimed that I was tailgating another vehicle, which I knew was not the case.

Soon four more patrol cars pulled up, two parking in front of my Expedition and the other two behind it. So now several police officers, one of them a black male, are getting out and approaching my vehicle. I explained to them that my brother and I were on our way to church and that I was a sergeant stationed at the Marine Base in Albany. When I mentioned that the Phi Theta Kappa sticker on my back window was for my degree in criminal justice and that racial profiling was illegal, the black cop started laughing. Another trooper said sarcastically, "No, we don't think you're a drug dealer, especially in a nice vehicle like this." He seemed almost to be disappointed. "Well," he added, "your window tint is too dark." I responded by saying politely, "I thought you stopped me for alleged tailgating." Embarrassed because he had nothing for which he could charge me, he gave me a warning for my window tint, and that was the end of our conversation.

The black cop and his partner walked off laughing all the way to their car. I knew the law and was not going to be intimidated or let them search my vehicle without a warrant because I had done nothing wrong. One thing I learned in college is that knowledge is power. I never thought that I would be using my education in criminal justice so quickly.

*Jermaine Jenkins graduates magna cum laude from
Hinds Community College in December 2001.*

Chapter 6

The Military and
College Continued

Hungry for more knowledge, I decided to go back to college in 2005. Living at the time in the Bahamas, I decided to look into online colleges. I found some good, regionally accredited colleges on the Internet. Some military officers I knew had received their degrees from online institutions, which led to them obtaining commissions. With my research complete, I enrolled into American InterContinental University and began my quest for a bachelor's degree.

Attending college online required a lot of discipline, initiative, and time-management skills. My homework consisted of three to four paragraphs each week in response to other people's comments on the topics of discussion for that week. By week's end an eight- to fifteen-page paper was due. This workload took a lot of my time, but I did not mind it at all. I quickly realized that online universities were just as hard as brick-and-mortar schools. When I was obliged to attend evening events hosted by the U.S. Ambassador, I would leave soon afterwards to get home and start on my homework. My friends in the Drug Enforcement Agency and Coast Guard also hosted functions at which I could spend only limited time because of my studies. Nothing was going to stop me from receiving my B.S. degree.

In my first few online classes I made B's before the A's started to roll in once I put myself on a dedicated schedule. My confidence continued to soar as I stayed focused on education. I was about two courses away from finishing my degree when I realized that I had a GPA of 3.3. My friend and mentor William Jones told me that I had to get my four-year degree with a GPA of 3.5 or higher. To make things more challenging, he advised me to start on a master's degree soon after I completed my B.S. William, I knew, was right, and his résumé spoke for itself. He and his wife Vanessa are well-known and highly respected people in Hattiesburg. Vanessa is a judge and has her own law firm; William has a J.D. degree from the University of Mississippi. So I buckled down, making an A- in one course and an A+ in the other to give me an overall GPA of 3.5. I had earned academic honors again, thanks to William Jones!

Life Learning Tip

Take advice from people who have been where you want to go. My mentor pushed me because he himself had worked hard to finish his bachelor's degree with honors, which in turn led to his being accepted at law school. If the person giving you advice has his or her life together, you need to listen. While emulating their accomplishments, come up with your own recipe for success. That is what I did, and it works! Everyone has to be a follower before he or she can become a leader. Let already successful people guide you. I guarantee that it will be a valuable and rewarding learning experience.

Special Article on College Education

In an article titled "The Importance of a College Education," Jeff McGuire explains that high school graduates today are unable to obtain the high-paying jobs that were once widely available. The U.S. has been transformed from a manufacturing-based economy to one based on knowledge, and the importance of a college education today is comparable to that of a high school education forty years ago.

McGuire also explains that a college education is important because it offers networking opportunities. The more connections you make during your college career, the more options you will have when you begin your job search. Once you have started a career, however, the importance of a college education has not been exhausted. Having a college degree often allows greater opportunity for promotion.

Special Article on Trade Schools

I mentioned earlier that college might not be for everyone. For people who do not want to attend college, trade schools are an excellent alternative. The website TradeSecrets.com presents a helpful article on trade schools.

Those who would like to attain experience in a particular skill and enter the work industry soon after their studies can always opt for trade schools. Across the world are many trade schools that teach different kinds of skills. These skills include automobile repair, cooking, laboratory medical technology, etc.

These students are trained in such a way that soon after their graduation they can land jobs with good pay. Technical education in a trade school is almost equivalent to college programs. Trade schools train students in the basics of particular technical skills.

At the end of his or her education at a trade school a student is awarded an industry-specific certificate. Trade schools are often attended by people who would like to grow in their existing career or advance to a better job. Classes are scheduled for evenings and weekends, enabling such people to attend without interrupting their job hours. Some trade schools also offer online programs. Please take advantage of these great programs.

Education and Salaries

The website EarnMyDegree.com gives a breakdown on education-related salaries. It points out that employers have increasingly used diplomas and degrees as a way to screen applicants. And once you've landed the job you want, your salary will reflect your credentials. On average a person with a Master's degree **earns $31,900 more per year** than a high school graduate—a differential of 105%!

Here are some average salaries:

- Professional degree $109,600

- Doctorate $89,400

- Master's degree $62,300

- Bachelor's degree $52,200

- Associate degree $38,200

- Some college $36,800

- High school graduate $30,400

Chapter 7

Why You Should Consider Joining the Military and Tips on Promotions

At my sister's house about two years ago I heard one of her friends say, "I made sure I had good grades in high school so I did not have to join the military." I was infuriated by her ignorance. Many members of the military have college degrees in math, biochemistry, civil engineering, aeronautics, accounting, business, medicine, law, and nursing. Moreover, although she does have a master's degree in sociology, my sister's friend has big student loans to repay and makes only about $40,000 a year. At the time I was earning $76,000 a year, and with a promotion in 2010 I make a pretty good living in the military. Civilians need to know this information so that their kids can receive good advice on career options after graduation from high school or college.

The military, obviously, can involve life-threatening danger. If you join the Marine Corps or Army, you likely will deploy to Afghanistan or Iraq, but this does not mean that you necessarily will be in dangerous situations. Most people who deploy there never leave a main base to fight or conduct resupply. Only about 10% of soldiers, usually those in infantry units, ever pull the trigger on their weapon in combat. If you join the military and choose a job in administration, contracting, or nursing, among other fields, you probably will never fire your weapon at anyone.

I have heard some teenagers and adults say that they don't want to join the military because people will tell them what to do. My buddy who was a Marine recruiter experienced this firsthand at a Taco Bell in New Orleans. He told the kid behind the counter, "Okay, you don't want to join the military because people will tell you what to do. I understand, but give me a #5 combo with extra cheese." When his lunch was served, he then asked, "Did you see what I just did? I gave you an order, and you followed it." Whether you work at Burger King, J. C. Penney, Sears, or wherever, someone will always tell you what to do unless you are the manager. Even then you still will answer to banks and stockholders when they have questions about the organization.

If you're going to be told what to do in most jobs, why not make a good salary, travel, and enjoy great benefits? Here are some quick tips for success in the military: do your job, be on time, stay fit, be positive, and respect your supervisors. Sounds like a regular civilian job, doesn't it? Everyone is not cut out for the military, just as everyone is not cut out for college. You have to find your own balance.

I am not trying to recruit you but to educate you. Once again, more people die in car crashes and other accidents than in Afghanistan or Iraq. Go online and check the statistics for yourself. You'll be surprised.

Tips for Promotions in the Marine Corps/ Attend The Marine Corps University

The Marine Corps expresses that education is extremely important to better yourself, your organization and the nation. In Quantico, Virginia, the Marine Corps University offers several courses for enlisted Marines and officers. These academies educate and assist all U.S. and some Foreign Service members in shaping their skills, as leaders in the world's most powerful military. These academies train and educate leaders of all ranks. Retired Sergeant Major Rick Hawkins, retired Master Gunnery Sergeant Kelly Scanlon and Master Gunnery Sergeant John Willis and their staff are great mentors who teach and advise senior enlisted Marines on the importance of education and mentorship.

Education is vital to being successful in the Marine Corps. If you have not attended certain military academies, you will not be promoted to the next rank. Do not misinterpret this as some sort of punishment, however; with the lives of your sons and daughters in our hands, we owe them educated leaders who can make good and ethical decisions when the nation calls upon us. I totally agree with the Marine Corps support for education. Remember, we are never too old to learn.

Chapter 8

Military College-
Assistance Programs

Many civilians as well as members of the military do not take advantage of outstanding educational programs offered by the Armed Forces. If persons on active duty want to attend college, they do not have to use their post-9/11 benefits right away. Instead they can use the Tuition Assistance Program (TAP) that allows a student $4,500 a year for college. Central Texas University, Park University, American Military University, the University of Maryland, and the University of Phoenix make sure that their tuition rates fall within the TAP allowance. You thus have an opportunity to obtain an associate's and bachelor's degree without touching your post-9/11 benefits. This a great program for enlisted men and women who cannot afford to pay back student loans like their officer counterparts.

If you decide to pursue a master's degree, you may need to start using your post-9/11 benefits because graduate school can get expensive, and TAP does not cover everything. However, you now can take advantage of a new resource called the Top Program. TAP pays half, and the other fund pays half. You are still going to college without relying on student loans. Nothing is coming out of your pocket. The only down side to the Top Program is that you lose a whole month of benefits for college. For example, if your graduate class costs $2,000, TAP will pay $1,000, and post-9/11 benefits will pay $1,000. Your monthly allotment under the G.I. Bill is $3,000. You will lose the other $2,000, which you do not get back for future use. Here is my advice. If you are on active duty, use TAP for your undergraduate degrees. If you are returning to civilian life, wait and use the post-9/11 benefits. These include a monthly stipend for housing and books plus full tuition.

Another program I highly recommend is the Reserve Officers' Training Corps (ROTC). All military branches have ROTC programs. The Navy offers some of the best programs in nursing, dentistry, and other medical fields. After graduating from an accredited university such as the University of Georgia debt-free, you will serve as an officer in the Navy for a period of four years as your payback to the service.

The Army offers scholarships to those just graduating from high school or to those already in college. This means that you could receive a two-, three-, or four-year ROTC scholarship. Military officers are highly respected both in and out of the services. The pay is pretty good, usually starting at about $45,000, and you have no loans to repay. When military officers get promoted, their salary increases are significant. You will not be disappointed.

The military's college programs cannot be matched by any civilian organization. Take advantage of them! Here are a few websites where you can apply for Pell Grants (FAFSA), ROTC programs, and other scholarships:

www.fafsa.gov

www.goarmy.com/rotc/scholarships.html

www.navy.com/joining/education-opportunities/nrotc

www.AmeriCorps.gov

http://nhsc.hrsa.gov

www.Scholarships4Moms.net

www.ClassesUSA.com

www.ClassessandCareers.com

Chapter 9

Embassy Duty in Kabul, Afghanistan

In July 2007 I was working as a Marine Security Guard for the Department of State in Kabul, Afghanistan. This was a one-year assignment. I found myself with some free time and remembered my mentor William Jones's comment that time waits for no one. I found a master's degree program at the University of Phoenix in criminal justice and started to pursue it.

The program was challenging. The graduate school's regulations stated that one had to maintain a GPA of 3.0 in order to avoid academic probation. Unwisely, I was skeptical. Upon completing my first graduate class with a final grade of B-, I was immediately put on probation for my next four classes because my GPA was around a 2.8. Terrified that I might be suspended, I stepped up my game and made two A's in my next two courses followed by a B+ and A- in the third and fourth classes. I was back in business. I worked hard to come off academic probation, and it required often staying up to 3:00 a.m. writing ten- to thirteen-page papers every week. When my friends asked me why I was so tired and couldn't hang out with them at night, I told them I was pursuing my master's degree and would not let anything get in my way.

Meanwhile there were a few scary occasions at the embassy in Kabul. One was a loud explosion that shook the building. I was in the middle of a course assignment but quickly grabbed my shotgun and ran to the main building to analyze the situation. Once everything calmed down, I went back to focusing on my academic work. I left Kabul in July 2008 with five courses to go for completion of my master's degree.

Life Learning Tip

One day two Marine Corps officers and State Department personnel were in my office for a meeting. When one of the officers noticed some books on my desk and asked what I was working on, I explained that it was a college course.

He said, "Okay. So you're pursuing an associate degree?"

"No, sir," I replied.

His eyes got wider. "Okay. So you're working on a bachelor's degree?"

"No, sir," I answered.

"Okay," he continued. "Is it a certificate program or something of that sort?"

"No, sir," I responded. "I'm five courses away from my master's degree in criminal justice."

They all just stared at each other for a moment. I noticed immediately that the conversational tone changed. *So this is how it works*, I thought. People respect educational ambition. Not many enlisted Marines have achieved master's degrees. I knew then and there that I was part of their world, and I loved it. I learned something new that day—namely, that if you want to be part of the club, you have to work hard to obtain your credentials.

Chapter 10

Returning from
Kabul, Afghanistan

After spending twelve months in Afghanistan, I returned to Quantico, Virginia, for a short stint, during which time I was able to complete two more courses in my master's program. I then was ordered to Camp Lejeune Marine Base in Jacksonville, North Carolina. Soon after I arrived there, I found out that my new unit was scheduled to deploy in Afghanistan for twelve months.

I was assigned as the Personal Security Detail leader for my commanding officer. My primary billet was with the Gunnery Sergeant. I helped to manage the quality of living for over 2,500 Marines. This assignment kept me extremely busy and included dangerous travel with convoys. I knew that this deployment to Afghanistan would make finishing my last three courses almost impossible. I therefore devised a proactive plan. Looking at my syllabi for these courses, I decided to download and print all the required materials.

We arrived in Afghanistan in March 2010 at a base called Camp Leatherneck. The Internet there at this time was slow, but I knew that improvements would come sooner rather than later. After three months passed, the Internet was a little bit better, and I enrolled promptly in a new course. Whenever I was tasked to go out on a convoy to resupply a unit or provide security, I took my books, laptop, and notes with me. After a three-day trip I would come back with most of my homework done for the week. Then I would stay awake in my office until 3:00 a.m.

to finish my thirteen-page papers. My friends and boss were amazed at my work ethic.

Even though there were days when we had to deal with improvised explosive devices or IEDs on our convoy missions, I stayed focused and eventually finished my last three courses. I remember finally sending off my last paper. My master's program had been completed, and I waited on my degree to be conferred. I sat in my office for a few minutes smiling, as if I had won the Georgia Lottery. I then decided to share my good news, emailing my entire unit that I had just finished work for my master's degree. Numerous emails came back from fellow Marines sending their congratulations. The C and D student in high school who became a father in the eleventh grade now had earned his graduate degree. Who thought this could happen? I did.

Ladies and gentlemen, I am living proof that if you work hard you can achieve anything. Success will not fall into your lap. You have to pursue it aggressively and be willing to make the necessary sacrifices.

Life Learning Tip

Once again, parents, encourage your kids to go to college. So many young people mistakenly think that they're not smart enough to succeed in college. I once thought the same thing, but through hard work and commitment I earned three degrees.

You first have to believe that you can do it. Then take the second step by going to the college's information center or, if you are in the military, the base's education center. These people will be eager to help you. Once all of your paperwork is complete, enroll in a course that interests you. Once you receive an A or B in that first class your confidence will increase, and then you are on your way to becoming a college graduate.

When I hear people say that a college education is impossible during financially hard times, I ask whether they have thought about getting a degree in an area that the country needs such as nursing. Most people tell me no. I then ask whether they have considered attending a trade school and getting certified as an electrician. Most people again say no or make excuses as to why they cannot enroll in school. Times are hard, I explain, because you choose to let times be hard. Make a move or get left behind. You can make $8.00 an hour or $30.00 an hour. The choice is yours.

I do understand that college is not meant for everyone. You can achieve success by working for Taco Bell, perhaps starting on the register and eventually becoming a manager. There is nothing wrong with working at fast-food restaurants. The secret is to work your way to the top. Strive for success and be willing to put in the work to achieve it.

Chapter 11

Meeting Presidents and Working at Embassies

In September 2004 First Sergeant Anthony Wade suggested that I go on special assignment as a Marine security guard. This job meant that I would be traveling the world and working for the Department of State at United States embassies. I would have top-secret clearance, guard classified information, and protect American diplomats. After applying and being accepted, I attended the Marine Security Guard School in Quantico, Virginia. I then was sent to the U.S. embassy in Nassau, The Bahamas, where I supervised the Marine security detail. We lived there for eighteen months. My wife and I rented a four-bedroom house with three and a half baths. It was great to have so much room. We later moved into another fantastic home that had a pool and guest house.

Not surprisingly, family members and friends visited us a lot. When my good friend Harold Moore and his wife Anitia visited during Christmas 2005, Harold asked why the doors on my vehicle were so heavy. I explained that we traveled in armor-reinforced cars for security purposes. He then inquired, "Who is this guy driving us to your house?" I told him that the man was my driver and that we had four of them, a gardener, and a maid. Harold was stunned. Later we took the Moore family to the magnificent Atlantis Hotel, with its underground aquarium, and toured the whole island. It was a great Christmas.

One day I received a call from my boss, John Darling, who told me that then Secretary of State Condoleezza Rice would be coming to the Bahamas for a short visit and that we would be assisting in her security detail. Having always admired this impressive woman's achievements, I was thrilled. On the day of her arrival my Marine contingent and I waited at the hotel for her entrance. I told the Diplomatic Security Special Agents to let us know when she arrived, but I guess they forgot. We were standing in front of the hotel's elevator when I heard someone say, "Hello, gentlemen." I turned around to see the Secretary of State. For about three seconds I stood there mute and then while shaking her hand said, "Good afternoon, ma'am." We then escorted Ms. Rice to her room.

A few months later John Darling asked whether my Marine cohorts and I would like to meet former President Bill Clinton. "Of course we would!" I replied. Once President Clinton arrived, we conversed for several minutes, after which he asked whether any of the Marines wanted our pictures taken with him. "Of course, sir!" was our enthusiastic response. After the photo session he continued to talk with us until his Secret Service Agents dragged him away because he had to fly to Detroit to meet former President George H. W. Bush at the 2006 Super Bowl.

By late 2008 I was working at our embassy in Kabul, Afghanistan. My boss, Bruce Thomas, told us that we would be handling security for the Democratic nominee for President, then Senator Barack Obama. As an African American male I was excited about the man who had a chance to become the first African American President of the United States. We worked hard in preparation for his visit. Our job was simple: we would be responsible for security in the embassy building where he would be speaking. I was working on the Internet when I heard people applauding so loud that I stopped what I was doing and joined the welcoming throng. The next day Senator Obama had a short speech to deliver. Some of my Marines were posted at doors; a few stood near him while he spoke; and I remained by one of the doors while listening carefully to his speech. At the end of it I presented Senator Obama with a special military-challenge coin from my Marine group. In return he exchanged coins with us. I now have in my possession a coin that went from the President's hand to mine. This was one of the most important days of life. While working at this American embassy I also met Senator Harry Reed, Senator Chuck Hagel, and Secretary of Homeland Security Michael Chertoff.

While residing in Kabul, I visited Abu Dhabi and Dubai on several occasions. In Dubai I stayed at the exotic Al Bustan Rotana Hotel, which has five-star restaurants, a shopping mall, and, believe it or not, a snow-ski facility. In Abu Dhabi I billeted at the Hilton Hotel, which was equally magnificent. I was amazed at how much wealth was flowing into this area of the world from oil.

The next embassy where I worked for a few weeks was in Lomé, Togo, in West Africa. Once there I was driven throughout the country to see some famous sites. In sharp contrast to Dubai's prosperity, Africans were walking around with large baskets on their heads, some ten feet in length. Some people there had no shoes and lived in abject poverty. No matter their condition, however, everyone seemed to be in high spirits. Never again will I complain about life in America. No matter how bad you think you have it, try visiting countries such as Africa and Thailand.

The last embassy where I worked from October 2008 to January 2009 was in Sofia, Bulgaria. My boss there was Gregory Davis, who invited me to several formal dinner parties. Once again I was in a new country, wearing a suit and tie, and associating with embassy staff members and other executives. I traveled all around Bulgaria and learned about its historical ties to Russia. It is truly an amazing country that I would urge everyone to visit.

Jermaine Jenkins shaking hands with Senator Obama at the
U.S. Embassy in Kabul, Afghanistan in August 2008.

Jermaine Jenkins with his Marine Security Guard Team and
Senator Obama, Senator Reed and Senator Hagel.

Jermaine Jenkins and his Marine Security Guard Team with Secretary of State Condoleezza Rice at the U.S. Embassy in Kabul, Afghanistan.

Jermaine Jenkins and his Marine Security Guard Team finishing up a security detail for Security of State Rice in Nassau, The Bahamas.

Jermaine Jenkins, Demarco Gates and Novak attend an event at the Ambassador's residence with Governor Jeb Bush in 2006.

Chapter 12

Exposure to Other
Countries and People

Travel beyond your immediate state or region! By doing so, you will gain priceless experiences for you and especially your children. When I arrived in Washington, D.C., in July 2006, I fell in love with our country. My wife and I first visited the National Mall. Not having had an opportunity earlier in life to visit our nation's capital, I was awestruck to be standing next to these memorial sites. We then drove by the White House and Pentagon. The latter was especially impressive because I saw some of the reconstruction after the terrorist attacks of September 11, 2001.

Life Learning Tip

Parents, expose your children to the world at large. If you do not, they become mired in local value systems. If all they are exposed to is drugs, gangs, and poverty, then most likely their lives will follow the same path. My own family is an example. Most of the men, in fact 99% of them, have been in jail for felonies and gang activities or languished in low-paying jobs. Guess what? Their offspring followed the same example. Their dads and moms never exposed them to a more positive environment, the result being a vicious cycle that continues from one generation to the next.

I have had the opportunity, thanks to the military, to visit or live in Thailand, Germany, Japan, Afghanistan, Iraq, the Bahamas, France, Spain, Kyrgyzstan, Ireland, Bahrain, Kuwait, Togo, and a few other countries. I loved traveling to all these places, exposure that expanded my personal and geopolitical horizons immeasurably.

The military, admittedly, is not for everyone, but it can be beneficial for the teenager who is not yet ready for college. Take advantage of a system that is a well-oiled machine and that will allow you to retire at age forty with a monthly check deposited into your bank account.

*Jermaine Jenkins in Phuket, Thailand for a conference in 2008.
This was a weeklong trip. It was my second time in Thailand.*

Jermaine Jenkins and his Marine Security Guard Team in Sofia, Bulgaria.

Jermaine Jenkins in Lome, Togo (Africa) with some local children in November 2006.

Chapter 13

Mentors: Everyone Needs One

Choosing a mentor can be one of the most important decisions in your life. When you select a mentor, be very careful. Not everyone can or should be a mentor. Don't seek guidance on finances, for example, from someone who cannot balance his own checkbook. Choosing an unqualified mentor can hinder your spiritual, financial, and mental growth. If you have a mentor and you are in the same place year after year, then either you are not listening to him or he is giving you bad advice.

When seeking a mentor, find a person who is in a position where you would like to be. Ask what he or she did to get that $100,000 annual salary. Ask if he or she is willing to give you advice and guide you there. Can you call him or her for guidance on big decisions? Your mentor may have experienced similar situations before. His or her insights can pay major dividends for your decision.

A good mentor will check on you from time to time to make sure that you are staying focused. You should also brief the mentor on your accomplishments along the way. Show your game plan to your mentor and explain to him or her how you will accomplish your goals. Let your mentor advise you on your plan. Listen carefully and make the best decisions for you and your family.

Fortunately I have some great mentors. Most of them are at the next level in terms of their careers in management, finance, education, and military service. For instance, my military mentors are usually at least one rank higher than I am. My financial advisors have a lot more money than do my wife and I. Moreover, most of my mentors have advanced degrees and some even doctorates. One reason for the success that my wife and I have experienced is our mentors such as Mayor Johnny Dupree, Ph.D., William Jones, J.D., Oddie Jenkins, Linda Swan, Howard Bouldin, Willie Heppard, and many more. We are a unified team in our struggle to make possible better lives for our children and the United States of America's future. I encourage you to do the same.

Jermaine Jenkins promotion to (E-8) First Sergeant in May 2010. First Sergeant Christopher Combs (left) and Captain Mark Burrell (right) are two of my closest mentors and friends.

Chapter 14

Financial Investment

I n early 2000 Sergeant Major Daryl Stilling asked me if I was investing money. I replied that I could not afford it, but that was not actually the case. At the time I was a young sergeant at E-5 pay rank in the Marine Corps who was trying to take care of my family and keep up with the Joneses. I had a nice vehicle with all the bells and whistles, on which I had spent about $12,000. Still I was broke and living paycheck to paycheck. I was not investing for the future. After listening to Daryl, I reflected on how many people I knew in their fifties and sixties who were still working because they had made poor financial decisions earlier in life. Most of these people wanted to retire but had to continue working in order to pay their bills.

Daryl introduced me to his financial advisor, and I have been investing money ever since. I began with small amounts, as little as $25, for the first few months. For those who do not have a financial advisor, you can open an account with such banks as Navy Federal Credit Union and USAA. I give USAA a slight edge in terms of investing because they counsel you over the phone about short- and long-term strategies and the risk factors of various mutual funds.

If you are in your early twenties, you can afford to choose a high-risk fund that promises substantial returns, but you also can lose money faster. The advantage of investing at a young age is that, if the market is down for a few years, you have time to rebound. This is why it is important to start contributing to an IRA as soon as possible.

Some people misguidedly allege that they cannot afford to invest any money for their future well-being, but they can by reassessing their current lifestyle. If you eliminate fast-food restaurants, cigarettes, night clubs, and other costly habits, you will recover extra money in your budget. Some friends of mine spend $100 per month, or $1,200 a year, on cigarettes. Examine your expenditures to see which ones you can eliminate or reduce.

Would you like to have the option of cashing out your IRA before age sixty without being taxed? If so, you could possibly have enough money to pay off your house, car, and kids' education. If you start investing at age twenty, you could have a million dollars in your account by age sixty. We have a 529 College Fund for my son. I plan to make sure he is financial savvy so that he can give himself and his future family the best opportunities for a good life and early retirement.

This is the American Dream. You can have it if you are smart about stewardship of your income. Prudent saving and investing are a must!

Investment Companies and Banks I Value

Charles Swab www.schwab.com
Edward Jones www.edwardsjones.com
TDAmeritrade www.tdameritrade.com
Fidelity www.fidelity.com
USAA www.usaa.com
Vanguard www.vanguard.com
T. Rowe Price www.troweprice.com
Ameriprise www.ameriprise.com
Invesco Aim www.invesco.com

Banks

USAA www.usaa.com
Navy Federal www.navyfederal.org
Bank of America www.bankofamerica.com
ING Direct www.ingdirect.com

Chapter 15

Keeping Up with the Joneses

In the late 1990s I was deceiving myself thinking that financially everything was okay. In fact, I was in debt up to my ears. I got into this marginal situation by striving to keep up with the Joneses. From my friends and family I had learned at a young age that it was okay not to pay bills on time, but to maintain an expensive car for the sake of status was okay, and not to save or invest money was okay. After years of insolvency and bad credit, I learned that this lifestyle is stupid.

People, stop trying to keep up with the Joneses. If you cannot afford a car, don't buy it. If you don't need another credit card, don't apply for it. Start paying your bills on time, and forget the night clubs, tattoos, rims, and other car accessories. Let the Joneses manage their households while you manage yours. Please learn from my mistakes. Everyone knows someone who is trying to keep up with the Joneses so smile right now and try your best to get them back on track if they are willing to listen.

Chapter 16

An Emergency Account

B efore starting to invest in long-term securities, you need to have a short-term emergency account. What is it you ask? The answer is a reserve cache of funds that you should have on hand when you need to pay unexpected bills. For a long time I avoided the necessity of such a contingency plan. However, when I needed money for two $300 tires on my Ford Expedition, I had to scramble to figure out a way to pay the bill.

Tired of being in such financial straits, I decided to start an emergency account. Once I got this account established, I kept money in it and never touched the balance until unexpected expenses arose.

I suggest that you start such an account immediately with a goal of setting aside $5,000. Start off with incremental deposits of $25 per month if you are on a tight budget. This gradually increasing emergency reserve will save you a lot of heartache and embarrassment when hard times descend, as they assuredly will.

Chapter 17

Managing Your Credit Score

In 2000 I attempted to get a small loan and was denied. This hurt my feelings. I knew that my credit was not good, but I didn't know that it was so bad. I couldn't get a piece of bubblegum on my credit rating back then. I realized that without good credit I would get high interest rates or be denied for the smallest of loans. I had to do something.

After deciding to get back on track, I went on the Internet to download my credit report. My credit rating was low, and I had numerous unpaid bills. One of my mentors named Mike Francis taught me that I could ask creditors for a settlement if I could not pay back the entire balance because of high interest rates. I now had a game plan. Every time I got paid on the first and fifteenth of the month, I would target a delinquent account. If the balance owed on it was too high, I would call to ask for a settlement. For example, if you owe Discover Card $1,500, you can call them and say you only have $900, and sometimes they will accept this amount to settle the account. This strategy will save you $600 to help pay off other bills. I used this technique to get my credit in order, and it worked!

If you are in major debt, do not pay half of your available funds here and there. For instance, if I had $600 and owed Sears $700 and J. C. Penney $400, I would pay off J.C. Penney in full. Here is the reason why, as I learned from a professional financial advisor. If you are already ten months late and the bill is in collection, another month will not make things any worse. Moreover, if you are paying $50 here and $50 there, you will never get your accounts paid off because of high interest rates. Concentrate on paying off one bill at a time until all your accounts have no outstanding balances. Then watch your credit score go back up.

You will know when you are back in good standing. A year after I paid off all my bills I applied for an American Express credit card. When the bank gave me a $10,000 limit, I knew I was back. The first thing I did was to call the bank and say that I did not need so high a limit. However, remember this: if you can manage high margins of credit, it looks better for you.

Generally speaking, try to avoid dependence on credit cards. They will get you in big trouble and ruin your life. Most people max them out while knowing they can't afford to pay back the accrued balances. If you want a nice house and car, pay your bills on time every month and stay clear of credit-card debt.

What Is Your Credit Score?

500-579 Very Bad Credit Score. You will have a hard time getting a loan. If you are able to obtain a loan, it will be at an extremely high rate of interest.

Example: Buying a car at an interest rate of 20%, which means you will be paying a lot of money back because of your poor credit score.

580-619 Bad Credit Score. You will get a loan with a high interest rate.

Example: Buying a car at an interest rate of 18%. You will be paying back a lot of money on the loan.

620-659 Average Credit Score. You will get a loan at a high rate of interest.

Example: Buying a car at an interest rate of 14%. This is still not good.

660-699 Above Average Score. You will get a loan at a decent rate of interest.

Example: Buying a car at an interest rate of 9%.

700-759 Good Credit Score. You will easily get a loan with a low rate of interest.

Example: Buying a car at an interest rate of 4%. This is good.

760-849 Outstanding Credit Score. You will get the lowest rate of interest possible.

Example: Buying a car at an interest rate 1.5%. This is fantastic!

Pay attention to your score and be sure to check it at least once a year.

Here are some things that do not affect your credit score:

1. **Age**
2. **Checking your own credit**
3. **Rent payments**
4. **Child-support payments**
5. **Bank overdrafts**
6. **Your income**
7. **Credit advice for financial institutions**

IMPORTANT ARTICLE ON CREDIT SCORES

"What Your Credit Score Is Made Of" by LaToya Irby **gives an excellent breakdown on what comprises your credit score and what affects it. She writes:**

Your credit score is a three-digit number that is used to predict how you will pay your bills. The score ranges from 300-850 and is calculated using your credit history information from your credit report.

When you make an application for credit, the creditor or lender uses your credit score to quickly make a credit/no-credit decision. This same decision can very well be made by simply viewing your credit report, but the credit score makes decision-making easier and less subjective.

While there are several different versions of the credit score, the most commonly used version is the FICO score (Read FICO vs. FAKO). Developed by the Fair Isaac Company, the FICO score is used by many creditors and lenders to decide whether or not to extend credit to you.

Because some parts of your bill-paying history are more important than others, different pieces of your credit history are given different weights in calculating your credit score. Even though the specific equation for coming up with your credit score is proprietary information owned by Fair Isaac, we do know what information is used to calculate your score.

Payment history is 35%

Lenders are most concerned about whether or not you pay your bills. The best indicator of this is how you've paid your bills in the past. Late payments, collections, and bankruptcies all affect the payment history of your credit score. More recent delinquencies hurt your credit score more than those in the past.

Debt level is 30%

The amount of debt you have in comparison to your credit limits is known as credit utilization. The higher your credit utilization – the closer you are to your limits – the lower your credit score will be. Keep your credit card balances at about 30% of your credit limit or less.

Length of credit history 15%

Having a longer credit history is favorable because it gives more information about your spending habits. It's good to leave open the accounts that you've had for a long time.

Inquiries are 10%

Each time you make an application for credit, an inquiry is added to your credit report. Too many applications for credit can mean that you are taking on a lot of debt or that you are in some kind of financial trouble. While inquiries can remain on your credit report for two years, your credit score calculation only considers those made within a year.

Mix of credit is 10%

Having different kinds of accounts is favorable because it shows that you have experience managing a mix of credit. This isn't a significant factor in your credit score unless you don't have much other information on which to base your score. Open new accounts as you need them, not to simply have what seems like a better mix of credit.

Chapter 18

Taxes

When I left Hattiesburg, Mississippi, in 1994 for the Marine Corps, I had just received my income tax refund. Since I had a child already and a full-time job, I received approximately $900 back. I thought I was the man. Everyone in my community then loved tax season and made plans to go shopping. Few people if any talked about investing their refund or putting it away in a Money Market Account or Certificate of Deposit. Income tax season is the real Christmas for many Americans, usually the poor and financially misguided, who spend their refund within a month after receiving it.

Worst Mistake on Taxes

You may have been taught to claim zero deductions on your W-4 form so that you would get a big tax refund at the beginning of the year. This is completely wrong! My financial counselors point out that you should always claim your dependents throughout the tax year, aiming to receive no refund at all. Why? You otherwise are allowing the federal government to make money in the form of interest on your hard-earned income.

Why not emulate the government's money-making strategy? Let me explain. I claim my three dependents on my taxes. I get all my earned income throughout the year and invest it in stocks and bonds via an IRA. By knowing how the government uses our money to make money, you can use the same method to secure your financial future. We all should apply these tips, for knowledge is power. Reap the benefits.

Stop Wasting Tax Refunds

Stop spending your tax refunds on frivolous things. Do not be an income tax diva or showoff who brags about how happy you are that it is tax season. This behavior merely indicates to other people that you have not managed your income throughout the year and that you need a tax refund to stay afloat. Be smart, people.

Brief Story about Taxes and Investing

One morning at work I heard my boss talking to a friend about taxes. They both were from states that imposed high taxes, and they hated this situation. The friend explained to my boss that he had changed his home of record to a state with no income taxes. He said that if your home state has been charging you $1,200 in annual taxes, now you would be receiving an extra $100 a month in your paycheck. This money in turn could be invested in an IRA to earn interest for you and not the state government. So this is how the upper middle class does it, I thought. Be similarly intelligent about your money.

Income Game Plan

Let's suppose you know that every month you run short of funds to pay all of your bills. Perhaps you continuously rely on family members and friends to bail you out of trouble each month. Stop this pattern of mismanagement and dependency. If you stick with my game plan, you will have a successful year after receiving your tax refund.

For example, if you receive a refund of $3,600 for 2012, deposit it immediately into a bank account. You do not want this cash burning a hole in your pocket. If you run about $200 short on expenses each month, supplement your regular budget with $300 a month from that banked reserve of funds, allowing an extra $100 to be spent on unexpected expenses, dinner, or entertainment. Your bills are now paid in full each month; you have a little spare cash each month; and, most importantly, you don't have to lean on anyone else. This plan works!

Chapter 19

Job Versus Career

There is a big difference between a job and a career. A lot of people have jobs but not careers. A job will give you a source of income and might pay all of your bills, but will it offer an IRA and healthcare benefits?

If you have a job, learning most positions in the business will make you a valuable asset. If you can help it make money, usually you will make more money. This is what you are looking for in a job. If you reach the managerial level, you could be offered good pay, better benefits, and more responsibility. The goal in every job you have should be that of striving to be the best employee you can be. Let's now consider a career.

Careers typically involve retirement plans, medical/dental insurance, and much more. This is what you want for you and your family. Careers such as nursing, education and the military will require you to serve twenty to thirty years before you can retire with full benefits. In contrast to a job, a career encourages you to compete and advance in your profession.

The career path can be more intimidating than the job path because it places more responsibility for advancement on you. Perhaps this is why so many people I know are reluctant to pursue careers in law enforcement, the military, law, or nursing. Such careers may be challenging, but remember to keep your eyes on the prize. Ask yourself whether you currently have a job or a career.

Chapter 20

Are You a Leader or a Follower?

All of us started as followers, but there are two types who remain in that category. The first is the person who is afraid of leadership, perhaps because he or she has a speaking problem such as stuttering. Afraid of failure or ridicule, such individuals would rather follow than lead. The second kind of follower is the person who shirks greater responsibility. This individual will not be promoted in his or her organization.

Some experts propose that certain people are born to be leaders. Professor Ron Riggio of Claremont McKenna College, for example, claims that leadership is a DNA trait inherited from dominance and social hierarchy among animals. I believe that social hierarchy shapes leadership to the extent that some are born into privilege and becoming a leader is expected of them. The Kennedy and Bush offspring are perfect examples. Because their parents are willing to use all of their resources to ensure that their kids follow in their footsteps, the children have a head start on becoming successful leaders.

In the animal kingdom the strongest creature dominates. Most leaders in the human sphere are well educated and well spoken. To be an effective leader you must know how to manage others. See, for instance, the following points posted on a website called "Future Visions":

- The manager administers; the leader innovates.

- The manager is a copy; the leader is an original.

- The manager maintains; the leader develops.

- The manager accepts reality; the leader investigates it.

- The manager focuses on systems and structure; the leader focuses on people.

- The manager relies on control; the leader inspires trust.

- The leader originates.

- The manager accepts the status quo; the leader challenges it.

- The manager is the classic good soldier; the leader is his or her own person.

- The manager does things right; the leader does the right thing.

Anyone who is willing to follow, listen, and learn can become an effective leader. Everyone has the potential for genuine leadership. Some have to have that potential pulled out of them; others seek leadership roles throughout their lives. I encourage all of you to pursue self-improvement and become a leader.

My Leadership Story

As explained earlier in this narrative, I was a follower for most of my years in school. After I completed Marine Corps Boot Camp, however, at my secondary military training I noticed that some Marines wore green, red, and black rank insignias, signifying our platoon's leaders. These young Marines were invested with the power to get everyone from point A to point B. They were treated with considerable respect and given pay raises as well as special privileges.

Because I aspired to reach that level, in June 1994 I told a newly promoted guy that I wanted to assist him in his duties while he taught me the ropes. He did just that, and my rank insignia changed to a black border. I now was leading fellow Marines and loved being in charge at this basic level.

I then volunteered for jobs that gave me more responsibility while still meeting all the fitness and marksmanship requirements expected of all Marines. For example, I asked to represent my unit on special promotion boards that deliberated on whether a Marine candidate would be awarded an accelerated promotion to the next rank. Requesting such leadership billets made me stand apart from my peers. Instead of picking up all the trash, I now was in charge of the guys who were picking up the trash.

I worked hard to become the best leader I could be by taking notes. I learned what to do and what not to do as a leader. We all make mistakes, but what counts is how you fix those mistakes and learn from them. My hard work led to my becoming the Marine Corps Logistics Base of Albany, Georgia, Marine of the Year and receiving accelerated promotion to First Sergeant (E-8). This is not to brag, but simply to record how a guy who made barely passing grades in high school and who stuttered when speaking in public eventually became a leader. You have to pursue success aggressively if you want your life to change for the better.

From left to right. Sergeant Major of the Marine Corps, Micheal Barrett, First Sergeant Richard Canal, First Sergeant Ronald Neff, First Sergeant Jermaine Jenkins, First Sergeant Derone Joplin and Commandant of the Marine Corps, General Amos. It was my pleasure to be standing within and next to these outstanding leaders in October 2011 at the Castle in Afghanistan.

From left to right. Sergeant Major of the Marine Corps Carlton Kent, Gunnery Sergeant Jermaine Jenkins and Commandant of the Marine Corps General James Conway. It was great to be with these outstanding leaders of U.S. Marines.

Chapter 21

Public Speaking

Public speaking is probably most people's greatest fear, but it is a crucial career skill. An article titled "Understanding Why Public Speaking Is So Important" posted on the Internet on September 4, 2006, lists some reasons why we all should strive to be good public speakers.

- Effective public speaking will allow you to make a difference in your business, community, and perhaps even the world. By sharing your information with others, you are better able to increase the impact of your hopes, dreams, desires, and goals for your life and the world around you.

- By learning how to speak effectively in public, you will be able to increase your own self-confidence.

- It's important because at some point in life just about everyone will be required to involve themselves in one type of public speaking or another.

- Facility in public speaking is a career booster. In fact, business-school alumni who attended the University of Minnesota placed oral communication at the top of a list of skills relevant to overall job success.

- Public speaking is a powerful way to make a good impression on others and to help bridge gaps in understanding and cooperation.

Life Learning Tip

Because I used to talk very fast, people often asked me to slow down. In addition, my Mississippi accent and pronunciation didn't make understanding me any easier. I knew that my speaking skills were not the best. I had to correct that deficiency if I planned to excel in my career, become a politician, and help others as a mentor.

I therefore joined the Jacksonville, North Carolina, Toastmasters International Club in October 2010, one of the best life choices I have made. Toastmasters is a non profit organization devoted to cultivating proficiency in public speaking and leadership. Members give speeches in front of other members and receive evaluation feedback from them. Members also are taught skills in collaborative team work.

I have given eleven speeches as a Toastmaster and earned the title of Competent Communicator. Nowadays when I speak in public to others I find myself speaking more slowly and using natural pauses. I have gained confidence in my skills and have spoken at six professional events. Toastmaster dues are only about $42 annually, which makes membership affordable to all who are seeking self-improvement. I encourage anyone who has a speech problem or who is intimidated by speaking in front of others to join this great organization and attend its meetings regularly. Toastmasters International gives you invaluable life skills.

Chapter 22

The Importance of Physical and Mental Fitness

America is being called the most overweight nation in the world. Some experts say that the problem is due to all the steroids used to produce food faster for consumption. Other experts say that it is due to more fast-food restaurants opening up on every corner. The restaurants make the food affordable, and the commercials advertising such fatty foods are designed to attract our kids and teenagers.

A lot of kids today are experiencing serious health conditions such as diabetes because parents don't take the time to cook healthy meals and get their kids involved in sports or basic exercise programs. If you as parents cannot afford sports activities, walking with your child in a park will keep him or her active and burning fat.

Children in the South in such states as Arkansas, Georgia, Kentucky, and Mississippi are showing much higher rates of obesity than their counterparts in other states. Mississippi has the highest rate of obesity. When the residents of this state are broken down by race and socio-economic class, disparities in obesity are extremely high in African American and Hispanic communities.

Obesity in children can lead to depression. In a study by Jeffrey Schwimmer at the University of California in San Diego, he reported that obese children rated their quality of life as low as did cancer patients. Overweight kids are bullied and taunted on a consistent basis. If you allow your children to consume fatty foods every day, you are a major part of the problem. You may think you are doing your child a favor, but you are really setting them up for failure.

Being overweight can cause low self-esteem and other issues. One study I read stated that 74% of men and 60% of women said that they would be uncomfortable dating someone who was obese. The French conducted a study in 2010 that found obese women to be 30% more likely than those of normal weight not to have had a sexual partner within the last year. Men also have a hard time finding a sexual partner when they are overweight, but the study did prove that their chances were better than women's.

The next time you are in a shopping mall, take five minutes to watch those walking around. You undoubtedly will notice the weight issue that our country is experiencing. We have to support First Lady Michelle Obama and reduce the number of overweight children in America. This is not about politics. It is about our taking care of the next generation.

African Americans' Acceptance of Obesity

African Americans have the highest obesity rates in the United States of America. Thaddeus Bell, M.D., conducted an online study about obesity in the black community. The study showed that 50.8% of black females and 28.8% of black males are overweight or obese. It also shows that black females and males exercise less than white females and males.

Many people contend that they do not have the time to exercise. The problem is that they do not want to take the time to exercise. Today there are no valid excuses for people *not* to stay healthy.

I have noticed these same issues with my family members and friends in Mississippi. Many of them do not exercise, and if they do it is a quick 20-minute walk one day a week. A lot of my friends' weight is ballooning out of control, and sadly they think it is okay. We all have to encourage each other to get out and exercise to stay healthy and live longer.

Obesity leads to heart disease, which is the number one killer of black males in the U.S. Black females will soon take the lead in this statistic if they continue to accept obesity as a cultural norm. Here are some reasons why physical activity is so important in our lives.

Confidence

Having a trim physique gives you confidence in the work environment and when dating. Your physical appearance is a factor in getting the job that you want. An employer knows that your being healthy means fewer doctor appointments and more business productivity.

Weight Control

Exercising will help to keep your weight low. When you exercise, you burn calories. It takes 3,500 calories to gain a pound. I advise people to drop from their diet 500 calories per day for seven days. This math comes out to one pound lost each week. Running in particular burns a lot of calories. You can start by walking or jogging. When you work your way up to running, you will be burning up to 500 calories per workout. Lose weight and look great.

Better Rest

After a hard workout and a full day of work, it is easier for you to fall asleep at night. If you are having a hard time sleeping, do a quick workout followed by a good shower.

More Energy

Have you ever walked up a flight of stairs and stopped to catch your breath when you made it to the top? Exercising regularly will give you the energy and stamina so that situations like this will not happen to you.

Improved Sex Life

Exercising regularly can also improve your sex life. Looking better usually means that your mate will want to be more intimate with you. And men who are in shape have fewer sexual problems such as erectile dysfunction.

Do not be the guy or girl who cannot find a date for the prom, a business dinner, or other social engagements because you are overweight. Too many Americans are starting to accept that being obese is okay, but it is not.

Jermaine Jenkins after a good workout in 2008 in Kabul, Afghanistan.

*Jermaine Jenkins starting on his 30 minutes of cardio. I do this
at least three days a week. Great fat burner. January 2011.*

Jermaine Jenkins getting ready to conduct strength training in May 2012. As you get older you must continue to exercise.

Staying Mentally Fit

You should always be seeking ways to improve your analytical skills. By being a problem-solver you make yourself more attractive to employers. This is the reason why math and science majors in college are so valuable whether the economy is good or bad. Here are some things I do to stay mentally fit.

1. Exercising is something we all need to do to stay mentally fit. Challenge yourself by doing new exercises. Your brain will also be working because you will be concentrating on completing the exercises you have begun.

2. Play problem-solving games such as word puzzles. They will stretch your brain in trying to figure out the answers.

3. Tell stories from a long time ago. As a member of Toastmasters International, I am always telling stories in my speeches. I often have to recall stories from ten years ago. This challenges me by making me think back as far as I can.

4. Supplements such as fish oil are good for your brain. You can buy these supplements for an inexpensive price. Walnuts are also a good source of brain food, but stay away from foods high in saturated fats.

5. Have people challenge you who are smarter than you in certain areas. Because my wife is a former math major and I am not good in math, I have her write out math problems that I try my best to solve. If I cannot figure one out, she teaches me all the steps and then writes out new problems for me to solve. This is a great brain-teaser.

6. Read more often. Reading helps you to learn new content material and vocabulary.

Staying mentally fit is something we all must do if we plan to be successful. I encourage you to read more books and seek out things to improve your analytical skills. Employers clearly value problem-solvers. Show them that you have what it takes to earn their respect.

Chapter 23

Parents Are Crippling
Their Children
"The Crutch, Bailout and
Accountability Theory"

Why are adult kids who are 43 years old still living at home with their parents? Why are adult kids still borrowing their parents car and do not own one? Why are adult kids still borrowing $10.00 from their parent's every other day? Why are your grown children failing and have yet to make strides in their lives and careers? I have thirty and forty year old friends and family members who have never held jobs and are still living at home with their parents. Most of them switch jobs every few months or years while moving in and out of their parents home. The answer to these questions is that you parents allow them to do it by always bailing them out of tough situations.

When children graduate from high school, most parents will support them through college. I agree with this concept and do this for my two daughters (Charmane and Quanisha) at this very moment. Teenagers who choose to do otherwise will most likely need a little time to get a job and find somewhere to live. This is an important transition time for our teens. I would concentrate on teaching them how to become a responsible adult and not depending on mom and dad for every little thing. All of this guidance and support is great; however, here is where the problem starts.

Parents are not letting their children mature and figure out things on their own. Parents are bailing their adult children out of every bad situation they encounter, not realizing they are preventing them from ever learning how to stand on their own feet. It's understandable that sometimes your adult children will need a little help every once in a while. However, when your assistance becomes habitual, it hurts them more than helps them. These adults are being crippled, causing them to become failures in life and that affects our whole country. There are parents who are struggling in their day to day lives with twenty-two and twenty-five year old adults living in their household who refuse to work but the parents still allow them to stay at home. Some parents are creating a society of lazy men and women who will depend on the system of welfare to take care of them for a lifetime. Parents must start to hold their adult children accountable and make them responsible for their own actions.

Although it may not be easy, I think sometimes, we as parents have to let our adult children hit rock bottom in order for them to learn from their mistakes. In addition, when mistakes are made, we need to stop making excuses for them. This practice is all too common within my own family. Enrique Ford, a good friend and mentor of mine, taught me something very important he called "The Crutch Theory". Basically, he believed if you continuously accept the irresponsible behaviors of your adult children and continue to loan them money, allow them to move back into your home, and bail them out of countless situations, then you would have become a crutch to them. People love to lean on crutches for support, however; when you pull that crutch from under a person they are forced to stand on their own feet, holding them accountable for their own successes and failures.

Parents, if you want your children to have a better chance of being successful in life, then please, do not become a crutch, stop bailing them out of every situation and hold them accountable for their actions. They are adults now and the more successful they are the better America will be!

Chapter 24

Preparing for the Mission in Combat and Life

I arrived at my new unit, Second Light Armored Reconnaissance Battalion, in July 2010. I knew before I arrived that we would be deploying to Afghanistan. At first I was not too happy about the assignment because I had already been on a one-year deployment with another unit.

Second Light Armored Reconnaissance Battalion has a rich history of doing a great job on assigned missions in combat. I knew we were going to be busy Marines during the upcoming and possibly dangerous deployment.

Military Classes for Deployment

Before military units deploy to a foreign land, they have to attend numerous classes on the country's geography, culture, and customs. Then begins actual training to achieve success. If you have poor training, you will most likely have poor performance, which can lead to failure in combat. No one wants to fail in life.

Civilian Classes and Training

Just as in the military, you have to prepare for your mission in civilian life. Devise a plan about your goals, how you will achieve them, and what obstacles might stand in your way. This should be a five-year plan. You want to make sure that you eliminate all or most of the obstacles that could potentially slow you down or prevent you from accomplishing your goals.

Upon Arriving in Afghanistan

Upon arriving in Afghanistan, service members are given refresher classes so that they will be prepared for the upcoming challenges. The goal is to keep soldiers in a problem-solving mode. These young men and women need to know how to make tough decisions quickly.

Such training allows military supervisors to evaluate their Marines and make sure they are ready to perform in the austere environment of Afghanistan. Supervisors also have to attend classes and training. They are given advanced training in most areas so that they can continue to teach younger service members throughout their deployment.

Upon Arriving at College

Classes and training for civilians are not unlike those in the military. Students need to work hard to maintain good grades, which are indicators of their future work ethic. The real test will come later once they are employed.

Rehearsals Ensure Success

Military units are given training rehearsals in the United States before deployment abroad. There is a well known saying that "practice makes perfect." In the Marine Corps we say, "Perfect practice makes perfect." We understand that things can change dramatically on the battlefield, but we strive to ensure that our young men and women are ready to handle any adverse situation.

Military Mindset for Success

Before soldiers are deployed, the military preaches about having a combat mindset. This means keeping your head in the game. You need to stay alert to your surroundings and remember why you are there in the first place. There will be times when every service member's mind drifts off to domestic situations at home. Such issues arise with every deployment, but a soldier's mindset must remain focused on the job at hand. By learning to work through issues and keep their head in the game, military members accomplish their mission and arrive safely back home.

Civilian Mindset for Success

The mindset of the average civilian must be focused on the prize. Whether a college student or business manager, you have to keep your mind in the game. You also have to learn to work through your problems and accomplish your goals. Remember that we all have problems in our lives. What makes us stronger is how we deal with the issues in front of us and how quickly we get our mind back into the game.

Put Everything Learned into Action

Now that you have been taught about a focused mindset, it is time to put everything you have learned into action. Soldiers will go on their mission to Afghanistan and hopefully achieve success. Civilians will go out into the job market and hopefully accomplish their goals. If you apply yourself and follow a five-year game plan, there is no reason why you cannot achieve your dreams.

Caption: From left to right. First Sergeant Jermaine Jenkins, Lance Corporal Peterka, Doc Carolous and Lance Corporal Bone. Just finished completing a successful mission in Southern Afghanistan and almost time to return to the great USA. October 2011.

Conclusion

I never thought while growing up that I was smart enough to go to college. No teacher, unfortunately, asked me whether I needed help in certain areas. I routinely failed math but made sure that I passed in my other subjects. We all have some learning deficiencies. The good news is that these issues can be corrected if parents identify such problems and assist their children in getting assistance. Most young people are waiting for an adult to help them.

It takes hard work to achieve your dream. Along the way nothing will be given to you. One of the biggest problems in the United States today is that too many people expect handouts. There is no such thing as handouts in well-paying careers. I mentioned earlier that if you want to be a success in life, you have to earn it. I did it, and so can you.

Most of us have been through hard times financially. Many of us have found out that money does not grow on trees. It took hitting rock bottom for many Americans to wake up and smell the coffee. I have shared some stories of personal struggles with finances so that you can learn from my mistakes. Pay attention to my tips on finances and don't fall prey to my past mistakes.

I once heard someone say, "Life is a game, and the quality of your life depends on how well you play the game." I couldn't agree more. When you think about basketball, the first person who probably comes to mind is Michael Jordan. The quality of his life is outstanding because he played the game very well. You may not have Michael Jordan's basketball skills, but we all have a talent and should work to perfect it.

Never let anyone distract or discourage you from achieving personal success. Always stay motivated and surround yourself with positive people who can provide assistance. If you feel like quitting college because an economics class is stressing you out, positive-thinking friends will be the people to keep you on track.

Qualified mentors will give you an honest opinion about any situation you face. Call upon them for guidance regarding finances, college, switching jobs, marriage, or anything else you would like to discuss. If you ask them how they achieved success, they will show you the way. Listen to their advice and make the best decisions for you and your family. Thank you for taking the time to read this book, which I hope has inspired you to scale new summits of personal success.